I CAN TELL YOU THE VERSION THAT WILL MAKE YOU TAKE MY SIDE

POEMS BY
J BROOKE

Independently published by *Driftwood Press*
in the United States of America.

Managing Poetry Editor:
Sara Moore Wagner
Cover Design: Sally Franckowiak
Covers & Interior Images: Ío Wuerich
Innards Design: James McNulty
Copyeditor: Sara Moore Wagner
Fonts: Rift Soft, Maecenas, Garamond,
& Merriweather

First published on June 2, 2026
ISBN-13: 978-1-949065-43-5
Please visit our website at www.driftwoodpress.com
or email us at editor@driftwoodpress.net.

PRAISE FOR *I CAN TELL YOU THE VERSION THAT WILL MAKE YOU TAKE MY SIDE*

"A beautiful book of poetry following one human's journey towards themselves, illuminating gender identity and the culture that surrounds us all—insightful and inspiring!"

— Rosie O'Donnell,
Performer/Activist

"Funny and surprising, a real gem."

— Hannah Gadsby,
Comedian/Writer

"The poems found in *I Can Tell You the Version That Will Make You Take My Side* are as intentional and full-bodied as the poet who penned them. J Brooke is a truth-teller with a gift for precise storytelling who walks the reader through the dark and light spaces of a life evolving, becoming anew."

— Amanda Johnston,
61st Texas Poet Laureate

"J Brooke's *I Can Tell You the Version That Will Make You Take My Side* is a book of rare courage—one that refuses performance, explanation, or any version that might win easy sympathy. Instead, these poems stand in the full, contradictory glare of memory and body, and say: I am here, I will not simplify what I carry. What lingers isn't a neat resolution but the stubborn dignity of survival—the daily, unspectacular ache of choosing to live honestly, with humor and care, even when the world demands a tidier answer. This is a collection that trusts the reader with what is unfinished and unfixable, and in doing so, offers something like hope—hope that we, too, might live inside our own contradictions and be seen."

— Morgan Talty,
author of *Night of the Living Rez: Stories* & *Fire Exit*

"J Brooke's poems absolutely blew me away. They are wise, angry, loving, gentle, and ferocious. I often had to stop as I read them to catch my breath, or to shake my head in wonder. Luminous, loving, and illuminating."

— Jennifer Finney Boylan,
author of *Mad Honey* (with Jodi Picoult)
& *She's Not There: A Life in Two Genders*

"With a humorous warmth that recalls Frank O'Hara, the speaker of J Brooke's *I Can Tell You the Version That Will Make You Take My Side* takes us down intimate streets along which we meet: a terrifyingly dysfunctional mother, many loved-ones the poet loves hard, negotiations of transness and self-acceptance, the pleasures of marriage. All while managing to offer up a wicked-strong dose of hilarity, Brooke's immaculate and intuitive lineation reminds us that the intensity of poetry, as a medium, acts as a sort of blood transfusion, helping us to feel our own veins out, so that we might better see ourselves in order to better see others."

— Cate Marvin,
author of *Event Horizon*

"In their courageous debut poetry collection, *I Can Tell You the Version That Will Make You Take My Side*, J Brooke examines the thorny question of gender. These deeply personal yet painfully relatable poems (to anyone with a body) are crucial to read in political moment when the rights of marginalized groups are being eroded and trans people are being targeted and demonized for being themselves. Brooke's collection is testament to the way art renders even sadistic executive orders—that fly in the face of the constitution, the courts, and all compassion—impotent. Although Brooke is known for their nonfiction and filmmaking, they are a new and singular voice in contemporary poetry."

— Jennifer Franklin,
author of *A Fire in Her Brain*

For Rose

CONTENTS

Any resemblance to specific individuals living or dead is unintended and not a representation of real people known to the author.

"I remember a field trip I took with my class in third grade...I took my shirt off too and walked in the shallows just wearing my shorts. ...My teacher intervened... I walked back to put my shirt on again. But I didn't feel that I had done anything wrong."

—Maia Kobabe, *Gender Queer*

"If you can be your own force of nature and have a positive heart, then you can actually do something good in the world."

—Eddie Izzard

I
WHY
I AM

DEMORALIZER

I can tell you the version
that will make you take
my side—but I'm not
going to tell you that
version. Instead
I'll offer this: I pretended
a secret then a beast
urchin burgeoning miscreant
untamed beggar thieving
manipulation absorbing cunning
weighing slaying
my captors

THIN AIR

In the closet
my father used
to use, I stand in
his shoes. He left
them all it seems
behind and I cannot
imagine what he is
walking around in socks too slippery—
sliding about, spilling
his cocktails, dribbling
cigar ashes. Barefooted, I
imagine him a boy
selling newspapers
at the corner of nowhere
and gone.

MISTAKEN IDENTITY

Dear Orangutan, I am
sorry I called out
"baboon" eyeing you
at the zoo. You must be
bothered being mistaken
for another
other than yourself.
Like me, you are
vegetarian, loner, devoid
a tail –
I do not know enough
though I suppose
when it got decided
that we get divided
by a single glass
pane –
someone mistook you
again.

EXIT STRATEGY

The very first time I consider ending
my life   I am four. Me
and my brother are permitted a walk

after dinner   (us leaving only
after folding our napkins and politely
requesting,   *may I be*

excused?) to explore resort terrain
in places   like Acapulco—
places that put jealous faces on teachers

when we go   back wearing tans,
delivering show-and-tell trinkets like leftover
pesos   and piñatas. We skip,

hop on one leg run fast along pristine paths
snaking   around spa buildings,
tennis courts, giant swimming pools. We

impersonate   a tightrope act, balancing
along floating docks yachts cling to by rope.
I stick   with my brother, older

by five years he is constantly checking his glow-
in-the-dark   Timex, deciding when
to turn back. This one night is different: I'm not

excused   to accompany my brother
on a walk. I'm excused instead to head to *the ladies*
room   (I only call it that to her—

to my mother or she won't allow me my exit)
I never   use that word otherwise
and never ever enter doors saying it. Instead,

I slip   into *mens rooms* or when on
vacations like this I'll use those bathrooms marked
rest   *room* next to the pool. Coming

back, I hear my brother whistling to himself, so I go
quietly   find him. *BOO!* I yell so
he jumps laughs chases me and I run then hide

behind   a tree. He is better at pretty
much everything, except not at hide-and-seek, or jax,
or red-light-   green-light 1 - 2 - 3 or

kickball or rope climbing. And if I hold my breath
when I hide,   he gives up, yelling, *Come out!*
Come out! Wherever you are! without ever finding

me. This night   after he yells *come out* I reappear,
begging for *one more time* so he covers both eyes and counts.
I take off,   running on grass instead of cement

so my patent leather shoes go silent. I head to the Pro Shop—
darkened   and closed at night— the headless
mannequins in tennis outfits attract but also spook me so

I try to look /   not look and I squint a bit and zoom
upstairs to the second level— open air, a canopy top and heavy
chairs jumbled   like cutlery thrown down a staircase

by folks dragging them into odd positions to watch tennis
matches   on the courts below. *Ready or not here*
I come shouts my brother, peeling hands from his eyes, walking

looking   behind trees, trying his hardest but not
even coming close to finding me. From my perch I see him
in a way   I rarely can— tippy top of his head

where his part divides his hair. So neat looking— impossibly
hard straight-   line side part like he used a ruler. I see
his Timex glowing (he wears it outside his shirt cinching tight

his sleeve   like a belt around a slim waist) super
unmanly my father says… Except my brother doesn't care
when anyone   says stuff like that, simply preferring

not moving his sleeve out of the way to reveal time.
My eyes   drool seeing the tops of his loafers
too— perfect shiny brown penny loafers I want to possess

so badly.   Instead of pennies I'd put pesos inside
those slots, but my mother says *maybe* to me getting a pair after
I outgrow   shoes I wear and hate. Pretty much wanting

everything my brother has and pretty much getting none of it.
Except if   his Timex breaks he'll get another, and
I'm promised his broken one. *Why do you want a broken watch*

not able   *to tell time?* Leni asks. *It won't matter*
I tell Leni *because I can't tell time*, I say. Really, I just want
to feel   the tight band squeeze my skin— feel

the burning metal heated by sun like what happens when I let
my teaspoon   soak in hot tea— I use it under the table
to burn my hand, singeing me a little, leaving a mark behind

on my palm   like a real tattoo like Popeye has. I don't
like Popeye, but I like sailor uniforms a lot— I like *I'm Popeye*
the sailor man   *I'm Popeye the sailor man…* that song

I hum to myself whenever I'm eating Alpha Bits or Apple Jacks.
I think it's crazy   I'm not allowed anything basically
every other kid gets to do, and yet I can make myself breakfast

from cereals no other kid ever gets to eat. Sugar
I appreciate but it can't stop me thinking about suicide. Not this
very first time on this vacation in Acapulco— while I'm

playing hide-and-seek with my brother I hear screaming,
Jimmy! It's my mother calling him *Jimmy!*
She just keeps screaming until he pops up like toast popping

out from the toaster— then he jumps to attention
like my GI Joe saluting *Yes?* My mother, still screaming, *Have*
you seen that sister of yours? My brother's head

darts side to side like a pinball desperate trying to discern
from where her voice is screaming. From my perch
I see her smoke first, clouding above tall hedges quickly

moving in our direction. Peering over the railing
to the tennis court below I know if I jump, I won't
bounce

like a
tennis
ball,

or even like a racquet hurled hard at the rubber
surface by older kids getting mad during lessons. I know
I will die quickly— upon impact, leaving my body

lying in a jumble like on CSI before the sheet covers the corpse
I imagine my blood spreading outwards, a fat puddle
all around me like red wine infecting a cocktail napkin when

the glass gets over-filled. I imagine my mother, still
smoking, looking down at me. Would she touch me? I wonder,
see if I have any life left in me? I decide she wouldn't—

instead, she'll have my father lift me up and carry me—
my corpse—   away to where? Where will my body be
kept until vacation ends and we all go home for my funeral? Why

I don't   jump this night doesn't matter. What matters
is I think something I can never unthink. That matters a great deal
to me.   Even if I didn't think about dying more

than other kids growing up in unhappy families, I now knew
something—   I now held the power to control one perfect thing
in my life— even if it ended up becoming the last thing ever in my life.

Now armed,   I was a fire fighter commanding infinite water
extinguishing violent flames. Later, while catching hell from my mother
I pretend-   fall asleep amidst screaming and my heart

pounding like it does when I'm in trouble. Except now, cushioning
my heart   beats as a piano damper pedal muffles sound,
floated this new, light, soft impossible freedom—

freedom   to get away, for good.
That carried me off to sleep this night, an angel
cocooning   me safely upwards.

I DREW A HOUSE

I drew a house
I drew a house with a tire swing
I drew a house with a tire swing and deep green grass
I drew a house with a tire swing and deep green grass
and a little pond

with a small raft afloat in it
and a mast in the center of it
with a blue bandana flag tied on
with sailor's knots

I drew a house
I drew a house with a tire swing
I drew a house with a tire swing and deep green grass
I drew a house with a tire swing and deep green grass
and a little pond

with sailor's knots I had learned from the encyclopedia
britannica in my brother's room
that I wasn't allowed to touch
without permission from my brother

I drew a house
I drew a house with a tire swing
I drew a house with a tire swing and deep green grass
I drew a house with a tire swing and deep green grass
and a little pond

without permission from my brother I couldn't get
because he was away at summer camp for eight weeks
or home late every afternoon after school
because he was busy with older boy things and I was not

I drew a house
I drew a house with a tire swing
I drew a house with a tire swing and deep green grass
I drew a house with a tire swing and deep green grass
and a little pond

because he was busy with older boy things and I was not
and there were no cell phones back then so I could never
reach him
when I wanted to which was most of the time
so I tiptoed into his room
and always took one of the many volumes of his encyclopedia

I drew a house
I drew a house with a tire swing
I drew a house with a tire swing and deep green grass
I drew a house with a tire swing and deep green grass
and a little pond

and always took one of the many volumes of his encyclopedia
and hid it under my shirt
and raced back to my bedroom, locking the door behind me
and crawling beneath my bed to read things with a flashlight

I drew a house
I drew a house with a tire swing
I drew a house with a tire swing and deep green grass
I drew a house with a tire swing and deep green grass
and a little pond

and crawling beneath my bed to read things with a flashlight
that would make me wish I could learn things
from someone besides myself
who maybe had a house with a tire swing

and deep green grass
and a little pond
with a small raft afloat in it
and a mast in the center of it
with a blue bandana flag
tied on with sailor's knots.

RULES TO AGE 11

Wash your hands after using the bathroom, *before* using the bathroom if you've been outside first, before dinner, after playing with any toys, instruments, or feeding your fish. Even if you're about to take a bath, if you've done *any* of those things, wash your hands first. With soap. Use the back door to come and go. Use the front door for guests. Ring the silver bell once only for Millie to bring something from the kitchen during dinner. Do *not* make a mess making lunch.

Breakfast can be any cereal except Count Chocula, but don't make any noise preparing it. Especially important *zero* noise getting ready for school so you don't wake mom. If mom is also asleep after school, don't make noise then either.

Don't talk about dad. Unless you want to talk about him in a bad way; then comments permitted and encouraged. Don't interrupt. Especially when mom is complaining about dad. Don't interrupt even if you think mom's not speaking, she's merely inhaling her Virginia Slims Menthol for a pause, and isn't done

speaking. Just wait until she exhales her smoke and continues what she wants to say.

Don't tell the doorman, the elevator man, the super, or the men in the garage to call you by your first initial. It's not proper they must address you as "Miss" even if it makes your throat burn and your skin itch.

Don't hide in the closet where dad left his stuff when he moved out. You're not allowed in there under any circumstances even though all you want to do is stand very still in his shoes, fish around his pockets for loose change, and smell hard the cigars still in the box.

Don't ask about sex. Don't ask about being Jewish. Don't ask about a psychiatrist, even though Richard Beenan sees one and says it's fun. Don't ask again about having a dog. Make eye contact. Shake hands hard, like you mean it. Speak in a clear voice. Read the news article taped to your bathroom mirror and be ready to discuss it at dinner. Do *not* mention the article if no one brings it up.

Sit like a lady. Walk like a lady. Carry a purse even though it feels like death. Let mom put lipstick on you even though you look like the Joker in *Batman* in it (even though you like watching *Batman* and think you could grow up to be Robin).

Stop slouching. Stop dragging your feet. Stop putting your hands in your pockets. Stop speaking in a low voice. Stop cracking your knuckles. Stop biting your nails short. Stop wearing your hair like that. Stop scratching. Stop spitting. Stop—no boys sneakers. No boys backpacks No short ski jackets No blazers with inside pockets No tube socks No aftershave No collars up No button-downs No button fly jeans Stop asking why you can't dress like Stop wondering why you can't be who you are.

GIGANTOR

At the day camp I'm sent, there's all this singing
I didn't anticipate. My family never sings that way

Leni sang me to sleep before Leni was fired.
Afterwards I sing myself to sleep every night singing

every song Leni ever sang me in bed. I sing in whispers
so I don't get in trouble like Leni did. Because I can tell

if I'm kicked out like Leni I'm too young to live alone,
on my own— I'm too young for a job. At day camp they sing

different songs than I learned from Leni, making me wonder
how long I'll pretend-sing before my brain remembers

all the camp song words. Most involve hand gestures, this added
layer of me remembering hurts deep in my stomach. But I don't tell

counselors because I fear them sending me to the nurse for that
pink medicine the nurse uses a lunchroom spoon for— the same

exact spoon— on each kid she makes take medicine. I've seen her
wipe it mindlessly using her sleeve or the paper towel it rests on

faceup, the spoon growing pink ghost streaks never evaporating
This is just one of many gross things disgusting me in the world

I first heard *disgust* — that word used—when my mother said it
about my father, and I liked that it sounded the same as *discussed*

(a word used a lot at home, that I like a lot less.) "We already
discussed this J, you're not to sit with Richard B at lunch."

That *discussed* concerns what I'm not allowed to do, but disgust is
something I feel about things, like that smell in the changing room

at camp. I'm the only one disgusted of course because I'm alone
noticing it while everyone else changes. I'm already changed—

wearing my swimsuit like a secret I hide under my T-shirt
when I get dressed in my bedroom before camp so I'm different

from the kids yanking and tugging damp underpants, hopping
bare feet on grass with slime oozing mud between their toes,

most kids are naked or half-naked and they never look happy.
Kids like Jed get red struggling, kids like Grace cry. And I

like swimming in the pool and I obviously love tag and
capturing the flag but I don't understand what they mean

when they yell: "free play," so that's when I just run
to the swings and swing so high my stomach flips

in a good way and I wish my life was all about swinging
and almost never about singing, and I mean I don't hate

"Edelweiss", but also don't get why we sing about this
"blossom of snow" in fiery July. I don't of course mind

"Itsy Bitsy Spider" because the hand gestures for it
are hard to mess up. But "Thumbelina" I despise.

"Thumbelina" disgusts me with those stupid
"you're no bigger than my thumb" stupid wave-

your-thumb-in-the-air hand gestures! Everyone stares at me
during it because they are all damned Thumbelinas while I'm

the one who isn't. I'm Gigantor instead. Gigantor the giant

robot from the cartoon my brother and I watched Saturday

mornings before older kids started singing at me
in the playground also in the lunchroom and on the bus

ride home. It's unfair because they sing the part that goes
"Gigantor" "Gigantor" "Gigantor" and then they sing the part

"Bigger than big / Taller than tall" before one of them can't
hold his laughter anymore, then everyone like dominoes fall

into each other all cracking up and becoming this huge
hysterical amoeba screaming "Gi-Gan-Tor, Gi-Gan-Tor"

at me. There's this other part to the Gigantor song though,
the part that goes "quicker than quick, stronger than strong.

Ready to fight for right, against wrong" but no one knows
that part except me and my brother, or if they know it

they don't bother singing it
after all the laughing starts.

BEFORE SURGERY

My nose *not mine to decide about*
is how mom explained signing me up
for surgery as if a manicure. I'd avoid

those, gnawing my nails biting deep
beneath the skin *Too short!*
said the manicurist dismissing me,

so happy then I couldn't even hide
my smile bannering my mug—smug,
I was, fielding mom's wrath in the taxi

flying up Madison making all the lights,
I wanted so bad to be our cab driver,
driving others, never being driven

like a leashed lap dog. But I couldn't bite
my nose, like my nails. Couldn't gnaw it
to a nub a surgeon would refuse

altering, citing insufficient material
to work with—I was stuck panicking
bargaining praying to god, offering

to stop cheating on math tests stop copying off
Lexi Mansfield who sucked at math,
though better than me. Lexi bore a dainty nose

my mom would have left the fuck alone,
never insisting on *fixing* involving violent striking
breaking shattering my bone the surgeon

warning I'd *hear it shatter deep within* me,
though I'd of course be *unconscious.*
I wondered about shattering my mom's nose

while she slept—if she would hear it—
cacophonous waking her, and would
it hurt her exactly the same way or worse?

JILTED

girlfriend— you were calfskin stilettos
red like your lips and cheeks

not quite sanguine
smoothed nylons caressed

taught "gams" parading passed desire,
the men and their dreams yearning

an impossibility. With me,
you were not fantasy nor veritas, never

something in a bottle you could atomize
anoint your intimate creases

with husbanded scents— lure
for a lover never arriving.

So out you go— me in tow, loyal
ballast, your trusted tenure

to theatre and ballet, openings
as if indoctrinations, primping

in rearview mirrors, dabbing
at lips lashes lobes, running

manicured nails atop coifed
locks, sprayed into submission.

I studied hard— every adjustment
of your skirt, miniscule belt cinched

in a flirt, you cajoling minions,
beckoning gazes, reeling in

your admirers before tossing them
back, leaving your hook in,

bloody souvenir. I was old enough
to couple then. Tall enough to squire

you through doors held ajar, me
following closely behind, observant

servant to your gait, your solo
waltz you'd dance. Every night,

a stage even as nighttime closed,
faded into light. Mourning

a lost lover, a silent suitor, a ghost
in absentia. Your waiting weighed

deep in my pockets like boulders,
me hoping we could skip

atop the water—*allegros, grand*
jetés above the surface before sinking.

Me imagining you afloat, always saving
you from sinking— rescuing you

before the inevitable drowning—
before I moved on.

WEAPONIZER

I can tell you the version
that will make you take
my side— but I'm not
going to tell you that
version. Instead
I'll offer this: I pretended
a girl then a young
woman using all
hair toss lip lick brazen
swagger wresting desire
from every man risking
my crosshairs

DANCE I DID

Beer bottle in back pocket, hips
        moving just enough,
arms adrift vectors on microscopic

gusts of wind. This is how I danced
        when I danced well. After taking in all
those beers I'd hold casually cocooning them

in my stiff Carhartt back pocket
        or in my loose Levi's,
keeping my eyes trained on someone,

momentary interest before shifting entirely
        away just when I make the connection
sever that invisible sinew connecting her gaze

to my gaze. And why the sudden disconnect?
        To confuse or intrigue or both.
And then that step that turns me away towards

Someone or no one — whatever whoever draws
        my focus obscured by my capacious self,
but not for long before a glide on the same side,

my smooth pivot back into place—spying through
        hair jostled loose, unkempt, pileated—
checking if I held that gaze.

MY AVATAR
(AKA AFAB PERPETRATES HETERONORMATIVE RELATIONSHIP)

My boyfriend used to complain I shed
all over his sweaters. Miles of my hair

brown strands slough without consent
adhering to him, and clinging fast as I

could not. The sinews of my love held
tight not to him and not to his beloved

two-ply Brooks Brothers' crew necks I
would steal and sleep within (lying not

entirely when claiming the softness so
elicited dreams I could not resist), only

omitting what became of my boyfriend
in my dreams. Not absent but present,

embodied by me, his nighttime avatar
floating through the world as I wished

to— hands casual in khaki pockets my
cologne, loafers, walk, talk, watch, just

the way I was born to embody, me just
the way I was born... like my boyfriend

only better. He would wrap scotch tape
around his hand, a tight concentric coil

of stickiness he engaged methodically
from left to right, patting himself top

to bottom, pressing homemade lint brush
to perform this preposterous display—

self-flagellation— a desperate pledge
of allegiance unable to locate the heart.

I told my boyfriend I loved him only when
he told me first. I did love witnessing him

treat my loosened locks like alien detritus,
like evidence, as if he were in on the secret.

BUMPER CARS

being the funniest
notion—pleasure
via violent collision—
deliberate accident
among strangers
allegedly safer

surplus rubber bound tight
all around. Sounds too much
like sex with men.

While female body
plus female body
always merging

versus colliding
languid surging
devoid of violence

fluid,
sacred,
sublime

floating towards locus
forgetting each carnival
ride comes with dangers.

II
NOT
GETTING
TOP
SURGERY

RATIONALIZER

I can tell you the version
that will make you take
my side— but I'm not
going to tell you that
version. Instead
I'll offer this: I pretended
a butch then a queer
duck donning disparate
feathers tags stripes trying
flying in vain
a flag to anywhere near
my self

I AM THE GULF OF MEXICO

See me my non-binary
gender
marker officially
disappeared January 20
poof
See the Black Trans
female First
Lieutenant two tours in
Afghanistan now not
anywhere See David Vizcaya
lost
mother Xiomara
searching for him,
pleading daily since
ICE
made a ghost
following
days detaining
maybe maiming
David prior to
erasing
on the official
detainee locator
online... at least we know
where Kilmar
first held in maximum security
terror
-ism confinement - is now. Our
supreme
court saying *Kilmar is due his*
due
process so bring him back with
supreme power

erased too   for a time
disappeared... or is it
back? Like Kilmar
like NPR
like NEA like
Department of Education not
known as DOE
which is otherwise Energy
and female deer depending
who you ask. But don't say
WHO
which is still
World Health Organization
where we don't belong
like we don't belong in Paris
Climate Accords
but if you went to jail for
violence
on January 6th you no longer
belong
in jail.   I don't
           belong
anywhere   anymore
           do I ?
I am Birthright Citizenship
University Autonomy Abortion
Rights
I am the USNS Harvey Milk,
           a shadow
of a former self   I am
           a Covid-19 vax
I am Gender Affirming Care
           looking
to affirm my gender anywhere
                      I am
a refugee seeking asylum

discarded
as a paper straw.
Am I ghosted
or residue? Will I
be brought back
will I be Stephen Colbert
will we all be
brought from a
brink or
be shadows dancing a
limbo
like I am? I am DEI
stricken poof
from websites like
USAID poof
after he said, *go and take your*
personal effects ASAP!
he said *GO!* In
English
as English now our official
language
in the US Español no longer
spoken here
¡Aquí ya no se habla Español!
like they speak in Mexico
bordering a Gulf
of America I am.

PRIVATE ALBERT CASHIER

Hi Mom, you're likely fuming   I'm late
phoning to check on you. You're sick
while I'm well into a
                                        Trans conference
learning how much I have in common
with Albert Cashier. Didn't you think it odd

as a kid I garbed in camo head-to-toe
rifle nestling into my shoulder,   saluting
Milly as she made beds, mopped, cooked
briskets, racks of lamb, aspic, artichokes,
she served us on a silver platter,
drenching

the uniform you made her wear. Unlike
Cashier, donning Union Army threads
of the 95th regiment. The shortest soldier,
            Albert
became wholeheartedly accepted
as "one of the boys" (this man knowing

a thing or two about bravery.) Fighting
in over forty engagements— one time
escaping capture   boldly overpowering
his prison guard—
            Cashier battled on
until the Civil War concluded. Albert

held various jobs after the war: church
janitor, farmhand, street lamplighter,
employee to a Senator,   (who hit Albert
            mistakenly with his limo,
                        shattering
poor Albert's leg.) Calculating the drop

from my fourth story bedroom window
I was a POW entertaining
jumping, only
my bedsheet parachute saving me, minus
a little partial paralysis, miniscule price
I gladly paid for my shortened sentence.

Cashier voted in elections, (as only men
could), concealing unwanted body parts,
he kept his secret
buried. Luckily the few
discovering his truth— doctors & former
comrades— all stayed mum. Embracing

my bayonet in bed, while poised beneath
my pillow a hidden toy grenade, or lying
motionless
zipped within a sleeping bag,
I'd hear distant melancholy taps serenade
me, imagining Milly carting my body out

with all your garbage. Albert lived to 71,
got buried in his uniform, enjoyed a full
military funeral with full military honors
his headstone reading: Albert Cashier, Co.
G, 95 Ill Inf.
until it got replaced. Of course

I'm phoning you now, late, feigning concern
for your health, not mentioning my disdain
for the women in 1977 revising poor Albert's
headstone to include his deadname. Probably
you knew these beasts.
I suspect you still do.

WHEN I CAME OUT TO YOU

When I bit Barbie's head off, when I stole Jim's racecar
pajamas, wearing them underneath. My baseball cap
seemingly surgically attached from kindergarten
through college I waged war whenever asked about

wearing tops on bathing suits. When I swigged Sprite,
imitating you drinking Heineken, emulating you
wiping the drips with my sleeve instead of napkin.
I wore a sweatshirt over two t-shirts both always stained

(one from mustard the other blood.) Hating you
teasing me, saying I wanted to marry Joe Namath—
yeah, no. I wanted to *be* Joe Namath and you knew it.
When I said call me "Sport" instead of "sweetheart,"

shoving my hands deep in my pockets, practicing spitting,
knuckle-cracking, peeing while standing. Toothpick in mouth,
sticking out, like a thug or a gangster. All those times begging
through a payphone for authentic cowboy boots, begging

for thick brown leather belts pleading for
LL Bean Black Watch plaid flannel, desperate
for a men's navy blazer— my holy grail—
the secret inside pockets where I'd conceal

a pocketknife, lighter, playing cards, marbles,
string. I used to write you from my bunk in camp,
with a flashlight write asking for a men's 10-speed,
GI Joes, sling shots, boxing gloves, Daisy Rifle,

boomerang, chemistry sets, erector sets,
a set of real walkie talkies to communicate
clearly, hoping I could be understood. I'd shave
my face stealing shaving cream you left behind,

slapping on your old aftershave, imagining
your big sandpaper hands bookending my face.
I'd thank grandpa whenever he'd chuckle at me
saying, "You could pass for a starting linebacker!" "You

definitely walk like Bucky Dent" said Uncle Stanley. My favorite
however, remains, "You move like a bull in a china shop"—
which mom said a lot, between her cigarette puffs describing me
to myself, forever making zero sense. After you left her,

leaving me too, alone fishing around in the dark for loose quarters,
dimes, nickels I'd save up, never spending. Your remnants, I saved
in this empty cigar box I hid under my bed. Keeping it wrapped in
tin foil, dropping it on your blanket in the end, coming out to you.

ON MY MIND

Denny having top surgery
the day after tomorrow is all
I think about. Simply nothing else

I can entertain. Not my writing
deadlines, hot water leaking
and the plumber rescheduling,

an inspection for the pickup
plus an oil change. I need to change
leftover candescent bulbs to LEDs

(harsher light, less energy) pick
wild asparagus before it grows
any taller— the cucumbers before

they grow bigger— rarely better
in vegetables— too thick, too sinewy,
too tough to ingest without spitting out,

small refusals balling up on the corner
of my plate. A lot like back when they
called Denny my "niece" though we

knew better. Denny, eating white food,
spitting out, rejecting their parents'
attempts back then to feed them,

not the eating disorder it was billed as,
more a control more a wish more like
I wished at three and five and eight

and twelve and sixteen and never again

after twenty until again after forty once
my parents were dead and buried, I tried again.

Dressing as a—moving as a—through a world
not wanting me changing, me finding change
too hard, the world too harsh. We all are too harsh.

To become ourselves, we must be brave
enough, strong enough, endure long enough
to be Denny two days from now. Chrysalis!

HEY TICKLE ME

Elmo at the dump (really
"recycle re-use" Lions
Club re-brand) so helpful
neighbors can share

their junk as treasure
a pleasure to drop
or take home much
like that wheelbarrow

I so wanted tho too slow
my roll... but lightning
quick I dumped mother's
mother's chafing dishes

"what's a chafing dish?"
asks my down-to-ground
spouse sourcing bamboo
toilet paper and lip balm

in cardboard tubes instead
of plastic. Mother's mother
a solid woman sporting
manly hands used to play

a hot fiddle, while chafing
dishes yellowed in a life
sentence without parole
in my mother's tobacco-

drenched classic six. Poor
original Elmo, drowning
daily in cigarette smoke,
enduring Lysol baptisms.

PACKER SHORT

Am I too old?   Nah,
I've yet to wear
my trousers rolled.
But   this morning
coffee in bed,   my wife
                                   and I scrolling —

Hers: prison reform plus
                                   longevity tips like walnuts
                                                  avocado and turmeric breakfasts
— Mine: social justice plus
          compression top binders
tanks and transmasc bottoms.

I swim   wearing nothing
          in private water, no one
sizing me up — not even
me. In public pools
                   I wear trunks and a top
                   or something Olympic
                   in nature,   cloaking at first
my afab frame,   before
soaking and revealing.

My algorithm, knowing
who I am,   hawks me
daily to   my gender core,
delivering this morning
          the packer short modeled
          on a body floating in a pool
          flaccid like what's packed
in that packer: slight bulge
a wet hint of a body part

you may not have. I don't

desire a bulge where
a penis I don't have
never grew.   A cock
I no longer seek,   a dick
I can barely recall ever
wanting— even back when
I practiced   peeing through
Slurpee straws repurposed
from my brain freeze blue
7-Eleven X-Treme Gulp...

There must have been
some blue slush stowaways
harbored inside those straws
turning my pee a happy green
stream. I remember   smiling

then, as I smile now seeing
                  another version of myself
at fifteen   floating through
a sultry afternoon wearing
nothing but packer shorts,
sipping my big blue Slurpee.

AREN'T YOU TAKING T?

My lunch friend queries
          (he, mid-chew mindless)
though my upper lip
ledge bare,   my hairline
          unfazed,   and he too
expert to make such a /

to misjudge   (top surgery
veteran) yet there it is
as if he knew me   better
than possible from text
/ emails dating back to
when we   both used They

/ Them. Funny,   voices
          don't change that way
you suppose they will—
his David Sedaris ping
-ing now off my steady
          Harry Styles— I track,

instead, his   evolving
author photos echoing
me as young me (baseball
capping kid)   bearding
          mustaching my face—
back when every print

or Polaroid I purloin
debase every magazine
face: Christie Brinkley
Sports Illustrated   swimsuit
issue   face,   Sally Field
People   Magazine

cover face, Margaret
Thatcher   Time   Woman
of the Year magazine
face... I hair them   all
bold   Sharpie wielding
micro-graffiti   artist

I was, always trans-
forming   every image.
          Yet once grown I stay
smooth, never chasing
late-day shadow   never
                    coveting wakeup time

pillow snag stubble
though folx   (like my
lunch buddy) misjudge
me regularly—   judge
an energy I exude akin
          to a chemical syringe

slipped beneath my skin.
Late for lunch, I hurried
reading his text directive
"blue shirt and beard"
          embellishing hairs   more
faint than I razor off

my toes.   Brandishing
a pink Venus shaver
my silken   wife   favors
balancing it delicately
on the edge of the tub
          we candlelight bathe in

submerged, nary an ounce
of   testosterone   between us.

WHY MUST MY COUSIN COME OUT?

Some whisper he should
only who really can tell
who is gay & who is bi
& who enby, mtf, trans-

masc, afab like me amab
like him maybe more fair
just to share *queer* & is it
the point even? The point

is my cousin—how hard
he works out that beautiful
body, stealing it away pecs
packed up to Pines on Fire

Island where he shares half
-truths he posts IG selfies all
food-porn but never *porn* porn
& friends, never lovers at least

never specifically. When arms
dangle loose around shoulders
in revealing drapes, he escapes
his head jerking or he smirking

awkwardly frozen his image
becoming a selfie of his false
self. I know you intimately
false self, embodied his age

this stage my cousin dares
perform on. I paced within
my own closet circles tight
concentric in darkness blind

-folded fumbling around so
bound groping for the handle
to a door held ajar by others
long before. *His generation*

is so free he should be out
and proud hisss those who
whisper within our family
chins lifted in silent gesture

in my cousin's direction. He
dances solo smiling sweetly
drunk at his brother's wedding
without a plus one, though he

is the best man. My cousin,
whenever/if ever he emerges
(like a damp chick victorious
and exhausted through shards

of shell) I hope he is deaf
to the straights singsong:
we knew we knew we knew
you all along! They sing

they know you. They don't
of course know, they don't
see as I see as I look at him
then look away. My silence

my salute to him, to myriad
incisions cleverly concealed
beneath tattoos, skin fragile
art, canvas for future pride.

FINITE DIGNITY

It's not that I'm catholic, though
I kind of like that organ music.
My only Vatican visit so far was
in worship of the Sistine Chapel

ceiling. Looking towards Adam
& his creation, I wonder about
those 1.9 centimeters separating
Adam's lazing fingers from his

lord's outstretched offering, rigid
& bold. Michelangelo conveying
consummate welcome yet leaving
space for what? Not rejection, not

considering the outcome, (we know
how that second act goes.) Did you
know Michelangelo— not *the* O.G.
his grandnephew instead, endowed

the identical name—altered his old
uncle's love poems, switching all
gender pronouns (male to female)
making Michelangelo appear less

queer. How many popes (you think)
staring up during sleepless wanders
wonder about Michelangelo and his
original intent... How many popes

pondering Michelangelo's sexuality
alongside artistry how many ponder
his gender? Pope Francis said Trans

folx could be baptized & Trans peeps

official godparents, he allowed them
official witnesses to catholic weddings
even Trans women made great pasta
dinner companions for Pope Francis

who invited them, sharing spaghetti,
laughter and his feelings *catholics*
should not alter surgically the body
god gave them. As if dignity is one

man's to grant another. Like that god
Michelangelo created, extending his
sure finger towards Adam who is still
deciding if he will return the gesture.

ONCE JUST ONCE I MINDED LESS ABOUT MY BREASTS

not caring while wearing my son
slung across   my torso   he clung
like a baby   leatherback   turtle
he would snorkel   alongside
a fistful of years   forward.
Born starving   nurses   warned
after   my   emergency   c-
section weeks before   a date
I'd been told   to expect him.
Wishing   for breast milk   asap
I fed him   instead
formula   a solution   born
of modern   healthcare   endorsed
by morphine   racing
through   my veins   like
rush hour   commuters sprinting
towards express trains   homeward
bound. To be a mistake,   something
must first   be.   My baby's first
cocktail   no less   an invention
to me   than me   a giver of life
a sustainer   through   my own
substance   my son   sustained,
his mouth searching   for a solution,
he being born   hungry   me being
born   a contradiction.
I walk   in a room   not a man
not a woman   I am   amalgam
contradiction   of both   cocked
head   jaw jut   to the left
towering   tall   shoulders   wide
rounded, a baseball   pitcher wound
tight. I'm   "mon"   in Caribbean
still   "mam"   down   south

almost never sometimes
my baby leatherback grown
swims in open water calling
me mom I pivot smile big.

LGB NO LONGER MY 4-LE ER WORD

Yeah I'm rans bu mos people can' ell.
Maybe hey can ell I'm nonbinary bu mos days
 hey jus misgender me "hey mam" (hough I'm no).
I was born his way, I always knew I was a boy
growing up bu back hen I was called " omboy"
which a leas had "boy" in he name. Puber y
blockers weren' a hing hen, bu   sex-change
surgery was and I ried every angle bu my paren s
wouln' buy i , so I s opped asking and grew up
wi h he wrong hormones coursing hrough me.
I looked like a sor of girl bu fel s ill so much
like a guy bu   hen over ime I admi I grew o
apprecia e my female hink bu s ill, I never did
adjus   o my body so I wear loose clo hing I wear
a rucker cap a lo (mos of he ime backwards)
and have never been a fan of mirrors bu I don'
wan surgery anymore because i 's surgery... and
I have already been hrough oo much. I 's a personal
decision o live (as I do, a " hey / hem) and I was glad
when hose pronouns became ubiqui ous
because hen I defini ely fel more seen. Bu of course
" hey/ hem" since he las elec ion isn' qui e as
accep ed jus like I'm no qui e as accep ed...
Presiden   rump said in his inaugura ion speech
I don' even exis ! I was in Canada during ha
momen so didn' hear him bu he said here are
only wo genders and hey are dic a ed by your body
a bir h. rump is mis aken on his, jus like he is
abou so many hings. He go rid of our rans flag
and he go rid of our le er " " in LGB   bu he can'
ge rid of me no ma er wha he akes away
or how he spells ha e.

PERSONAL ISSUES WITH TOP SURGERY

Scrolling Instagram in a bathroom
          (mindless avoidance my old friend)
seasoning my days callousing agile

fingertips while I pray not my heart
          as well. Oh hell, how awful my life
when my algorithm disappoints me

like this day, streaming royal family
          reels I didn't search for. I barely care
these whiter than white billionaires

spew & skew racist. I watched them
          fictionalized on Netflix— a version
so well-acted, so well edited, so well

my nosy phone eavesdropped, ratted
          me out so now I'm stuck scrolling
princes I don't care about riding

horses I don't care about so *hide*
          content I hit (tho adorable animal
scrolling I of course like conveyed

as ♡ but too many cats and hardly
          enough bears if you ask me.) I used
to spew "my spirit animal is a bear"

before updating— me appropriating
          at best & racist at worst making me
more royal I guess than bear-like...

I'm really most similar to teen boys

on my feed fooling around jumping
around horsing around in jeans often

shirtless their defined torsos liberated
strong cut perfect except for the scars
those damn scars remaining evidence

road map tracing backwards to where
their femaleness got removed— knifed
away like a branding— I consider scars

always considering my brand & if I can
handle such branding... I'd love myself
so much more in a t-shirt, except bare-

chested I imagine myself exposed still,
averting my eyes whenever passing
mirrors or windows reflecting like I do

now, always folding my arms covering
my chest, in photos I post I imagine it
my symbol of strength (only in reality

my symbol is hiding) still hiding always
hiding out— like I do in bathroom stalls
stalling as I do, as if behind palace walls

not a pretender— I have come out & out
& out again, so how is it I remain
still in hiding?

T

Maria hates olives. Jason vaunts a signature
cocktail, though never grilled a portobello.
Oral allergy syndrome is why Elizabeth eschews

raw apples. So many things I don't know
about my friends until I do. Until I see them
reveal something miniscule they suppose

of course, and it's not. Like with Jason,
his darkness is he stole something big.
I know, Jason never told Maria even

about being a thief, and they've been married
over two decades. Only I was told which makes me
feel like he knew I'd love him no matter what,

and even if I didn't feel that way before he told
me about his theft, I felt so protective of him after
he trusted me I can never think his signature cocktail

makes him a jerk— I know it's just something he creates
to cover up that part of him he believes *is* a jerk,
the part that's a thief even though he only acted

on it once. I carry around stuff like that all the time—
Like the way I think of myself as a murderer even
though I've done it literally— never. But so many times

I dream I'm disposing of body parts, stuffing
an arm into a cereal box, a leg into a garbage bag
and hauling them around to different garbage dumps,

recycling places, deserted landfills and murky swamps.

I know, you suppose, I get ideas like this watching TV shows
like *Dexter* but I don't watch those types of things, instead

I watch sweet funny fluff lighthearted romps
with precocious kids— I've been watching those shows
my whole life wanting willing myself

into ping-pong basements swing-set backyards
uncomplicated *Brady Bunch* houses I mean, so what
life growing up approximated *The Sopranos*? It's like being

double-jointed, in that, sure, you have something about you
different from most people but who really cares, like truly
gives a damn because in the end it's just something you schlepp

around with you like the rest of your shit. It's how I feel
some days about being T (as in the last letter in LGBT),
and not telling the friends who still think I'm the first letter

in LGBT. There are days the difference as significant
as the difference between being a murderer and just dreaming
about murdering. But there are plenty of other days I think

it's as insignificant as why my friend Elizabeth doesn't eat apples
meaning obscure medical diagnosis aside, isn't it absolutely enough
to just know not to offer her an apple?

CANCER SCARE

That's how I know for sure I don't
want top surgery I of course want

the outcome come out flat smooth
skin I want the reflection I always

squinted into mirrors hoping to see
myself reflected outside a loose tee

shirt beneath button downs ajar like
curtains loose layers layered looser

I pull again and again yanking poor
innocent fibers imploring they offer

impossible space for me to hide I'd
toss them all begin a fresh downsize

to medium or small jettison my soupy
slouchy swimmy threads dump donate

or burn the motherfuckers I desire that
outcome if only I can just blink it onto

me, awake to hands exploring my torso
my flat smooth chest no longer breasts

inhaling exhaling proudly satisfied and
yet I don't get it that surgery   I do not

choose surgery I do not elect it fearing
instead the scalpels needles anesthesia

I wonder was it the tonsillectomy I did
not need, elective surgery I didn't elect

at 4 when I didn't get a vote or was it
that rhinoplasty at 17 against my will

still no vote no voice my body bones
and skin I had in the game no control

like my uncle Stanley punctured at 42
by drains tubes liquid in and liquid out

emaciated once handsome stud I loved
visiting him that last hospital time that

could have done it But the lump under
my arm in my armpit (even my lymph

nodes avoid my breasts) so scary one
doctor calls another for a favor to see

me *See them today it's important*
please and I go and they poke

and avert their eyes frown prod
order the MRI ASAP as I dress

recalling all those times I begged
god please don't give me cancer

don't make it cancer anything
but cancer but if I must cancer

god, please breast cancer then
radical bilateral removal   not

elective but *medically mandated*
dissolution solution my problem

But I skirt death again the tests show
the lump is just some something acting

up inside me, a minor revolt I need no
surgery so I won't get surgery and I live

on in the body I was mistakenly wrapped
inside Unwanted gift to myself I remain

OUT LATE

So yeah, I know it feels late
telling you this I mean sure
me having had a trans kid—
pretty grand omission right?

Hear me out on this particular
elephant room-sauntering—
it's not like K appeared trans
all his life just different to me

in *a takes one to know one way.*
Really mostly we were flipping
pancakes, carting K & his sibs
to basketball, soccer, jujitsu, art

music lessons same as any other
attempting non-dysfunction fam
with queer parents navigating
difficult weekend fathers and K

adamantly hetero before lesbian
-leaning finally realizing he was
he so we jumped right in helping
transition along the way sourcing

gender affirming medical care
ushering K through changing
his legal name birth certificate
driver's license passport under-

wear hoodies socks watch razor
shave cream deodorant hair gel
nose piercing even warranting
a shift. I admit having post-op

post top surgery squeamishness
changing his drains, thankfully
his brother A, trained as EMT,
rescued us both, so I got away

only double knotting trash bags
filled with blood-soaked gauze.
K asked me to edit most family
and childhood photos he looked

not masculine in, so I cut them
up tiny before igniting in a fire
pit fire burning K's old bras too
as we celebrated ashes tangoing

across our lawn while Sia sang
Chandelier loud out of the blue-
tooth speaker K knocked over
reaching for his third Herradura.

Wild joy like that night needs to be
protected, so I tuck it tight. Bind it
close to my heart—never risking it
being diluted by a big gender stew.

SUPERMOON

Apparently I missed it—*once*
in a lifetime comet—just last
night. This happens so much

so many people I know care
like my sister-in-law chasing
those northern lights claiming

bucket list motivations—that
and her husband (my brother-
in-law) dying unexpectedly un-

mercifully makes fleeting
everything especially sky
miracles like eclipses—

solar and lunar—one thing
obscuring another entirely
or partially isn't that alone

worth it? The looking out
the looking up the looking
beyond ourselves. Ponder

whatever appears greater
than your immediate self
and your body disappears

entirely I tell myself passing
my reflection again illuminated
beneath yet another supermoon.

NOT FOR EVERYONE

She has taken to facing me
when sleeping... a good sign

I figured when it first began
late last August (the deep breath

in our summers) after visitors
dwindle, after our children

get their fills of our good-
wills, after we celebrate

our birthdays, each of us
one day apart from each

other—sharing dual days
like a weekend—a double

feature our simultaneity,
further evidence of our pairing—

a sublime predetermination.
We expertly share: one sink, one

hairbrush, one Netflix, one data
plan. Seven thousand three

hundred eighty-six dinners, still
counting. Rare nights we slept

alone—without the other tugging
gently at the duvet or tiptoeing

towards middle of the night
bathroom visits—can be tallied

on one and a half hands. Nights
not always facing breath to breath

exhaling years outlined by stress
I view those years now as lifeless—

as unrecognizable corpse strewn
within chalk outline, a crime scene

in a cold case no one wishes solved.
More than most things, I desire

these nights now; gentle tranquil
limbo we float inside. Ignoring

outside imagery beckoning me,
(imagery requiring surgery)

I choose, surprisingly, my own
mistaken form instead. That one

thrust onto me at birth, cruel
costume, zipperless dress—no exit

from my misgendered self, devoid
disturbing our tender universe.

HOW CAN ONE'S WORK NOT SUGGEST PROTEST IF WE ARE DEVOID A DAILY NORMALCY?

A CONVERSATION WITH J BROOKE & SARA MOORE WAGNER

First, welcome to the *Driftwood* family! We are very excited about having your book join our catalogue. Through our conversations, I know that *Driftwood* has been a dream press for you. Could you tell our readers a little about your connection to *Driftwood*, and why you feel we're a perfect match?

Thanks so much Sara—thrilled to have my debut book published by *Driftwood*. Your immediate use of the word "catalogue" is exactly why I was so hoping to go with your press. I don't recall exactly when *Driftwood* first occurred on my radar, but it began reoccurring when I became the Book Reviews Editor for *The Rumpus* and started collecting interesting independent fresh viewpoint presses. Again and again I'd be impressed with titles like Robin Gow's *Lanternfly August* and Xiang Yata's *Optometry*. I have those sorts of overflowing bookshelves you'd expect a writer and editor to have, but I purge and curate frequently to beat back the bedlam, and I find myself hanging onto a number of your books for various reasons.

You have a background as a nonfiction writer. When do you know when something works better as a poem? How did you come to poetry? Does your nonfiction work inform your poetry in any way?

See? That question is a huge reason I feel so at home at *Driftwood*! Often, because I write poetry, I'm asked to be seen exclusively as a poet, to answer questions as a poet... which makes me uncomfortable. I see myself as a writer, not specifically "a poet". I know lots of poets, and I believe there's a profound difference—viewing and interpreting the world exclusively through poetry. But those of us who are writers, I believe, think in one language and then express those thoughts through different dialects.

You ask how I "come to poetry" and I think the answer would be "sporadically, repeatedly, significantly." I wrote a poem when I was very young, maybe five or six, which won some national award. Then I didn't write another poem until high school, when I would scribble tortured teenage verse in black felt tips on scraps of vellum I'd crease small and stuff into my brown leather wallet. Then I went back to prose. About a decade ago I did a reading of an essay I wrote at a writers' conference and Billy Collins came up to me afterwards and said my prose was very poetic and I should take a class with him, so I did. A couple years later I asked him to write a recommendation letter for me for my applications to grad school. I was applying to various creative writing MFA programs but then one of them (largely due to Billy's letter), offered me a partial scholarship and said I could attend that semester instead of waiting six more months if I made my concentration poetry, so I did.

Following graduation, I mostly wrote and published prose. And then in 2024 I wrote this book, though some poems have their roots in 2019 when I completed my MFA and, in the process, evolved my pronouns and legally changed my name.

I wrote about my evolution in an essay titled "HYBRID" which was awarded first place in *Columbia Journal*'s Special Issue Nonfiction Prize. I went on to publish more essays weaving my gender through cultural commentary, and yet I turned to poetry to tell this story in the depth I needed to tell it.

For me, poems are the form I use when distilling my thoughts into imagery that floats.

2024 feels very significant here! Was this book difficult to write, emotionally or otherwise, especially in such a short time?

It was significant in that I sat down every day to write this book. I gave myself permission to write this story as connected poems instead of prose, and that felt significant too, that decision vs. a vacillation of form. The material is difficult to think about, but therapeutic to write about, if that makes sense.

2024 also feels contextually significant. Your book is often overtly political in the best way. A lot of poets have spoken about the intersections between politics and poetry. Poetry has always, since even before Plato, had a political function, whether it's backing or supporting governments or actively defying, which yours is doing, especially in poems like "I Am the Gulf of Mexico," where you challenge and name policies very directly. In a blog for the Poetry Foundation, Christopher Soto said, "If everything is political then maybe I don't like political poetry. I want protest poetry." Your poetry feels like exactly that: protest poetry. What is your view on what a political or protest poem should do? Do you have any political/protest poets who inspire you?

So my first course in grad school was supposed to be taught by the great political activist poet Martín Espada, but something sudden happened in his life, and he was replaced that semester by someone else... I felt somehow fate had sidestepped me, so I made sure to read a lot of Espada's work on my own, and even now, if I'm anywhere Espada is reading, I always attend. Perhaps proximity to that sort of voice subversively influenced me, but I don't know... I am a huge fan of Maya Angelou whose work was obviously the essence of political and protest but perhaps born in a different time and space her work would have reflected something else?

Personally, I have never defined myself as a political or activist writer, certainly not on the order of Christopher Soto who clarified, when asked, that his work isn't "sad" but rather "masochistic." I think I'm more a present-tense reactionary writer. I largely reference current or recent culture—so really, I'm writing about immediate environment, and the one we are all awaking to these days is so heightened politically, the writing ratchets up... I think a lot of writers are encountering a similar pull... look how frequently poems in *The Atlantic* or *The New Yorker* have that edge and how that didn't used to be the constant. How can one's work not suggest protest if we are devoid a daily normalcy?

In earliest 2025, upon reading the inauguration speech the new president of my country made, announcing my gender no longer existed, I was inspired to write the poem "I am the Gulf of Mexico." Shortly thereafter I wrote "LGB No Longer My Four Le er Word", I added these two poems to this collection, and it finally felt complete. So I think this book is political on two levels: certainly with the overtly political poems, but also the ones simply explaining my existence—because the best way I know how to fight erasure is my willingness to illuminate myself in as honest a way as I can.

The idea that you're "a present-tense reactionary writer" really pinpoints how your work feels so immediate! Related to this, do you hope your book or words inspire your readers to immediate action in any way?

Always. I'm just a believer in whatever anyone can do, they should. I have a sister-in-law I'm so proud of who is currently (as I tell her) "saving democracy" but I cannot organize and advocate and phone bank like she can—so I write, and I hope others write or bake or think or whatever. And those who only can leave the country and try to regroup from afar, I think that can be its own form of helpful too—I don't think it's surrendering to expat if that's what's needed to continue to think and breathe and be.

What does your drafting and submission process look like? Does it vary depending on your genre or the immediacy of the work? What advice do you have for other poets who are looking to speak through the silences happening now?

My work varies entirely based on the project and genre. I currently have a chapbook that is very specific in its politics ... a couple well-respected publishers have loved it but cannot produce it with the immediacy it would require... everyone says self-publish which would be the way to go for immediacy, but I absolutely don't have that sort of bandwidth right now for the follow-through, the promoting and distribution... I think people don't realize how much publishers take on and do! One of the reasons I don't have that time is a project I'm working on which is less immediate and culls a lot of my prose work from the past few years. I think when a project is ready, it's helpful to let experts read it—I like all sorts of readers, not just professional writers, in terms of feedback. But, like with so many things, I don't feel expert enough to give advice to poets on their process or work (if a poet wants to know where to stay in Montreal during a U.S. inauguration, I can be helpful), but I would say time, when it's an option, is generally a friend to great work.

This book deals with hard and potentially triggering subjects and images. From the beginning we see your speaker's childhood thoughts of suicide and the evolution of this related to feeling gendered pressures. It has me thinking about K. Iver's "Family of Origin Content Warning" poem in which they say, "This poem doesn't know/ why it must tell you. It wants you/to resist brightsiding its tragedies." Does this relate to why you wanted to explore these triggering subjects and images in detail? What do you want your reader to understand?

I think very young children naturally contemplate their own death. Early childhood games almost always involve playing dead. Mark Twain had Huck Finn imagine his own funeral and then attend it. I want to remind my readers of that, and both remove the curse of the adult overlay of suicide and link the notion of the child yearning to solve the painful portions of their world however they can imagine doing so. Children have almost no power except inside their own minds. So the contemplation of controlling one's own death is a very powerful place for a child to take their thinking. In the K. Iver poem you mention, concepting suicide is linked to sexual abuse, in my poem "Exit Strategy" it is linked to the child's most basic core self being negated. In both cases the notion of suicide is a way for a child to regain a power that has been taken away.

A clear theme of this collection is gender, what it means to the speaker and the outside world. Nonbinary and trans identities and lives are being actively erased currently. This collection not only allows the reader to understand the speaker's relationship to gender, it also invites the reader to enter the body of the speaker in the way only poetry can. Was this one of your main goals when crafting this collection?

Absolutely! Thank you for articulating that this exact way. I have written queerness into much of my work, but while it's sometimes the topic, it's just as often the wallpaper. My goal has never been to have an exclusively queer audience, but rather to deepen the general audience's understanding of queer people... and specifically here trans/nonbinary people. This goal is anything but lofty and is entirely selfish. Like most minority voices, I simply wish to be easily understood and, as result, accepted – not merely on the page but at the grocery store, at the airport, at the gas station.

Throughout your childhood poems, there's a motif of familial wealth. As someone who grew up poor, this element was fascinating and illuminating to me. Class feels very related to the way gender presentation/appropriateness was forced on the speaker. Was this something you were thinking about while writing these poems?

While in no way can my adult self romanticize growing up poor, as a child I sensed there was a vast fluidity permitted when self-invention was part of the aspiration. Whatever version of the "American Dream" paradigm one buys into, its fantasy is economic and class mobility and that allows for envisioning and then becoming—there's inherent conceptual freedom of self within it. My parents had wealth but that landed them in environments where appearances and maintaining appearances mattered a great deal, and there's inherent rigidity to that. For instance, my mother felt my father had too much body hair to blend in at their country club, so she made him shave his chest and back, but (for some reason) not his arms and legs... so at the swimming pool he resembled a grizzly bear wearing shorts and a tight burlap sweater vest—early evidence, to me, that keeping up appearances can turn you into a carnival act. So yes, when one is safeguarding appearances at all cost, any variant to sexuality or gender norms becomes potentially catastrophic. That was most significantly how our families' privilege impacted me negatively. So in this book, the boundaries of privilege contribute to the speaker's misery—but I'm careful to avoid making privilege its own misery in and of itself—that's insane and the speaker in my work, even as a young child, knows the distinction.

I'm also thinking about language theory as it relates to gender. I am always reaching for what Virginia Woolf called "the female sentence" in my own writing because, as feminist scholar Catharine MacKinnon said, "there is no ungendered reality or ungendered perspective," and that really sucks. Mainly, the current perspective is fiercely patriarchal and being pushed towards that more and more. Many of your poems and sentences are unique and experimental. Is the ungendered (or even AFAB?) sentence or reality something you are reaching for here?

I may need to return to grad school to feel equipped to answer this level of academically astute erudition... I always assume my "voice" is laden with the complicated gender fractals coursing through my brain. I write the way I think and my "think" is an amalgam of my intersecting genders, both biological and adoptive. If I felt I were coming off at all patriarchal I'd be horrified and shift—but anything else, any other genderish construct I allow.

Could you tell me more about where your experimental style comes from for you? Is it shaped, in any way, by other writers you love (who our readers may also love to discover!)?

I think my style comes from a background in multiple formats —that old poetic prose / prosaic poetry thing again... but I love any form that really surprises and also does the hard work communicating. I think what Carmen Maria Machado's *In The Dream House* does is brilliant and the essence of original. I'm a big Claudia Rankine fan and *Don't Let Me Be Lonely* blows me away every time I read it and I read it a couple times a year. I love Gabrielle Calvocoressi in general and learned a lot about form in their *Rocket Fantastic.* Layli Long Soldier's *Whereas* remains breakthrough. I just finished Taylor Byas' *Resting Bitch Face a*nd the book is bold in the variety of forms she uses, for instance she uses erasure in a very fresh way, and she has a couple things I believe she invented. Likewise, Spencer Williams' debut last year, *Tranz* is wonderful in general but notable for the many stylistic chances it takes – there are forms or the expansion of forms I believe are unique to this work.

The second half of your book beckons, often, to the next generation. I love how the speaker talks about their child and the difference in the approach to parenting, compared to your own early history. What do you wish the next generation would understand or realize, or even do differently?

My spouse and I released a feature documentary in 2009 about five people who came out (gay, lesbian, trans) for the first time during their senior citizen years. It was prior to Caitlin Jenner coming out, prior to the legalization of U.S. marriage equality, and prior to so many other massive LGBTQIA legal and cultural shifts and strides. At every film festival where we screened the film and did a Q and A after, an audience member would invariably ask what I wished for the next generation... I always said I wished my kid's generation wouldn't know what it means to "come out"—that that would no longer be a necessary thing because this would all be so commonplace pedestrian as to be a big fat *so what*. Sixteen years later this remains my main wish. But now I guess it's for my (so far nonexistent) grandkids' generation.

That's a beautiful dream, and let's hope it's sooner! I also write about my children and myself in often frank ways, and I'm always asked what they might think when they read my work. It's my hope they'll see only love there (I deeply see your book as about love, too!). How do you think parents should approach writing about their children?

There is so much being written now about how parents should and shouldn't approach using their children in their art. Sally Mann has apologized for the work which made her Sally Mann. John Cheever's daughter and Lucien Freud's daughter have both released books emphasizing how their lives should not have been mined as their parent's intellectual and artistic properties. I always admire the way authors like Anne Lamott navigate writing candidly about her kid and his struggles, but I think she does it from having thrown herself so deep under the bus that it somehow works. I remember hearing Mary Karr being asked about writing a lot of shocking material about her family during her book tour for *Lit: A Memoir* and her answer was "my teenage son doesn't care about my writing, he cares about my pancakes" and at that time it made sense to me—but that too was pre-Caitlin Jenner... There was a great deal of discussion surrounding this when I was a grad school student in 2019. When I went back to teach a few years later attitudes had shifted. I have been both careful and have made mistakes. To me, it's like seed oil, which a few years ago seemed an innocuous ingredient and now I stay the hell away from. I've repeatedly re-written the acknowledgments section to this collection, unsure whether to omit some of my kids, all of my kids, use their initials only... so I probably am not one to offer advice on the subject. I've dedicated this book to a young cousin of mine who is currently still a minor. I asked her parent's advice and permission —but while I mean the dedication to honor her, she may eventually find this an overstep – in which case it becomes just that. The ethical bridging of my truth and another's privacy is absolutely an ongoing conundrum.

You make so many great points here. I think I reconcile myself with it by thinking about truth and beauty—to erase the reality of my existence as a mother in my poems would be to erase a part of my identity, and the beauty in a part of life that's often seen as precious or "lesser." In an interview with the *Chicago Review of Books*, Maggie Smith said that when she began writing about her children, she was "well aware of the cultural bias against 'mommy poems.'... [she] overcame that by integrating the different parts of [her]self." Did your work change when you became a parent? Have you encountered this bias against poems about children in the literary community?

Every cell of my being changed when I became a parent—really overnight, like St. Augustine falling off the donkey I was a different person moments after giving birth—so my work changed as well. I think in many ways becoming a parent opened me up emotionally in ways which helped my writing; I became a more honest person, so as result a more honest artist. I have not encountered bias in the literary community that I'm aware of due to becoming a parent, to the contrary I found outlets like *Mom Egg Review* for poetry written by parents. But as for "mommy poems" I don't know—I mean Kate Baer has great work and a huge following, but her subject-matter has the underpinnings giving it credibility, it isn't just leaning into heartstrings. But there's also plenty of mediocrity out there masquerading as heartfelt that has a following, and there's a market for everything—who thought Labubu would be a thing?

The way you talk about social media in your poem "Personal Issues With Top Surgery" has me thinking about how much we hide and reveal, and the limits of always being "seen" in a curated way. Maybe we need poetry more than ever, especially poetry which pushes beyond those boundaries and bares all. How do you approach social media, and do you think social media is useful for artists?

Like my previous answer, this is very much an evolution for me. Years ago, during a time when I presented female, I broke the gender ceiling at the NYAC—a private athletic club in New York City—becoming one of its first "female" members. Years later, when I married Beatrice and requested a spouse card (something wives of male members were historically automatically given), I was turned down. While New York recognized our international marriage, marriage equality wasn't yet a federal right and my club used that against me. It took me hiring an attorney, spending $1,500 and briefly involving the ACLU to get my club, where I had been an exemplary always-on-time dues-paying member for over a decade, to issue my spouse the plastic 3-inch by 2-inch card granting her access to the facility. After that we had a choice, I could resign or we could make our presence known, modeling and normalizing our queer presence in the pool, sauna, gym, and tap room. It wasn't nearly as comfortable being the face of difference as quietly fading from the scene of the crime... but we did it and I'm not sorry we did. Similarly, while I keep my distance from things Meta and Musk, I haven't cancelled my IG and X accounts—showing up occasionally vs. promoting my own erasure by simply ceasing to exist on the sites. If I disappear myself, how am I helping the cause? And yet, it kills me to perpetuate, even in my miniscule way, the wealth and success of Zuckerberg and Elon. I migrated to Bluesky for kinder gentler reasons, but more converts are needed! I got Gabrielle Calvocoressi to open a Bluesky account, but they still post regularly on IG and only sporadically on Bluesky. Alexander Chee is on Bluesky, but not with the frequency he is on IG. And I gravitate to what thinkers like Chee and Calvocoressi have to say. I have liked accessing TikTok for short filmmaking things, so artistically, yeah...but it getting sold obviously will change how it's curated. The good news is high school kids are embracing retro—VHS, MP3, cassette tapes... they are hanging out in brick-and-mortar libraries and bookstores. So there's hope! I figure they must be writing poetry – scribbling tortured teenage verse with black felt tips.

I love that you have multiple poems that gesture to the title, "I can tell you the version that will make you take my side." Can you explain this a little more for our readers? What made you want to structure your book in this way, and what version of the story do you imagine WOULD make your reader "take your side"? Do you see each of these sections as an argument or explanation?

It's somewhat of an expansion on that old Winston Churchill line about history being written by the victors. He was referencing that those who win have the capital and means to tell the story future generations will come to believe as truth. But of course, that version of truth is often grossly inaccurate. Sometimes good historians like Howard Zinn come along and offer a truer picture. Every so often media gate keepers allow someone smart like Nikole Hannah-Jones to spread reality by truthful contextualization of American history in *The 1619 Project*. But then there's massive backlash—if half of a population believes one thing and half believes the polar opposite, spin becomes the order of the day. Writers know spinning words a certain way engenders head nods, nurtures support. (It's why writers are hired to put the words in the mouths of politicians.) I want to make transparent the self-awareness of the power to convince in my work—I want to acknowledge that I know what the relationship between writer and reader is and that I am trying to hold it to a more sacred standard through my willingness to expose the unseemly in myself, in my motives and actions. If a reader does end up taking sides, it's my hope they arrive where they do through deduction rather than seduction.

What's next for you?

As I mentioned, I have a chapbook that's timely and political seeking a publisher who moves quickly (know anyone?) I'm completing an essay collection for a different interested publisher (aka there are lunches but no contract yet). My job at *The Rumpus* takes up time—but I genuinely love the people, the work, marrying writers to books, engaging with those impassioned about being part of the literary community, and of course the excitement of new releases. I always say, "I'd do it for the ARCs alone," which is the truth.

ACKNOWLEDGEMENTS

"Finite Dignity" *Slippery Elm*, 2025

"Exit Strategy" (published in essay form as "The First Time I Consider Ending My Life I Am Four") *Room Magazine,* 2024

"I Drew a House" *The Rumpus,* 2023

"Rules to Age 11" *HerStry,* 2022

"Gigantor" Allen Ginsberg Poetry Awards section of the *Paterson Literary Review*, 2026

"My Avatar (aka afab perpetuates heteronormative relationship)" *Holy Gossip*, 2024

"Private Albert Cashier" (earlier version published as "Self-Portrait at Age 9 as Albert Cashier") *The Arlington Literary Journal*, 2021

"Bumper Cars" *Beyond Queer Words Anthology,* 2021

"T" *The Rumpus*, 2023

THANKS

I hope the folks in my sphere to whom I feel immense gratitude experience my thanks beyond this page. But those mentioned below are the ones who haven't received a bottle of scotch or an Edible Arrangement recently... the ones who make my writing life possible. Some of them even make it probable.

Thanks to my birth family for extensive early material... and especially to my brother James for continuing to process it all with me, because I know you'd rather watch the edited footage.

Thank you, B, E, K, A, L, M, (J), my subsequent family of seven, for enduring this career of mine.

Thank you specifically to my son Arthur for your brutal honesty and tender heart. My fervent wish is to leave behind work that either makes you proud or is simple to burn.

Thank you to my poetry writing buddies and peers Dr. Cynthia Scheinberg, Teri Elam, Jennifer Franklin, who read and respond to my early-stage work with rolled-up-sleeve honesty rather than praise.

Thank you to my prose writing buddy Morgan Talty, for the early-stage reading, erudite analysis, creative foul language commentary.

Thank you to Cate Marvin for teaching me the line. Thank you to T Fleischmann and Porochista Khakpour for teaching me to cross the line.

Thank you to Billy Collins for hearing me read my prose aloud and telling me to take your poetry class. Thank you to Roger Rosenblatt for reading my poetry and encouraging me to stick with prose.

Thank you to Lou Ann Walker, Amanda Johnston, Debra Marquart, Elizabeth Hand for supporting my earlier work far more than it deserved.

Thank you to Lauren Langston Klein and Morgan LaRocca at *Milkweed Poetry Press* and to Charles Carlisle at *Ashland Poetry Press* for the early-stage encouragement of this book, it really helped.

Thank you to Judith Weiss for shoving Randy Newman's lyrics down my throat as the poetry it is.

Thank you to Maria Baum for Umbria.

Thank you to Lisa Greenberg for you-know-what.

Thank you Melissa Bank for everything, I miss you.

Thank you Micah G. and Jen E. for setting an impossible-to-rival example of parenting a gender nonconforming child. If the billions of folx like me had just had either of you guys as parents, we could write very different books.

Thank you to Bob Levenson, Don Siegelaub, Uncle Lou – I miss each of your unique versions of tutelage wrapped in unconditional love and tossed generously in my direction.

Thanks to my childhood besties who stick around for my adult revision: Elizabeth H., Jason M., Cynno, Maria R., T... and for further extending your steadfast support of my work by willingly appearing in it.

Thanks to my close friends who sustain me by allowing my utter transparency (you guys are the dry run for my stories before the page): Jill & Bruce, Lor & Jess, Debby G., Lina & Terry, Elka R., Andrew P., Adrienne K., Carmen A., Pam M., Eliahu K.

Thanks to David G. (& Analee), David F. (& Melissa), Ross H., Katherine L., Jane & John, Eric & Lee, Jenny & Bob, Katie W., Jean C., Kim S., Andrea G., Stacy S., Molly C., for lightning-fast responses to specific and obscure questions whenever I drop in from the abyss.

Thanks to my queer literary buds: Jendi Reiter, Spider McKnight, Heather Jones, Jackie Domenus, Kelz Smoot for disappearing the white noise of being other whenever we connect. Oh, and Teri Elam— without whom I wouldn't have made it through grad school.

Thanks to Hannah, Marin, and Tony R. — my Gen Z and Gen Alpha cousins, you inspire me with your always fresh perspectives and overall riz, keeping it 6 7.

Thanks to Tony H. (who early on dubbed himself my "writing fan boy") and Pam W., the family I am so lucky to have gotten back into my life. And to Monica and Reg, the family I am so lucky to have been able to keep in my life.

Thanks to the young people I'm fortunate to have moving through my life, those commonly known as family and those I write in: Charlie G., Elle & Daphne, Jake C., Scott & Crisi, Jenya & Nick, Adam R., Harper, Rose, Tess, Gabe P., Owen, Ben W., Haley & Justin, Lexi, Hilary M., Gavi, Jack M., Tori, Ollie, John L., Brooke G., Rhi, Sabrina M., Luke C., Luca, Asher, Ariel & Nicole, Rennie, Maddie, Elliot G., Shayla L., Violet, Nick D., Jenna, Erin. You are each a glorious rebuke of the unconscionable mess of a world you've been handed.

Thanks to my assistant Aelen for so many things including the endless permutations of my TOC.

Thanks to Lori R., for many years of (far too often emergency) website, graphic, and miscellaneous tech help that really no one else could or would deal with.

Thanks to Acree Graham Macam who has been my student, my asst. editor, writing peer, book reviewer and friend, and who has been outstanding in each of those roles.

Thanks to Maribel for being a constant and astute reader of my work in your second language.

Merci to my Montreal tenants Cedric and Elodi who pay their rent on time so I can write instead of chasing you down. And thanks to Jesse F., Janne L., Annette V., Mark S. for keeping it safe.

Thank you to the many generous editors at publications who previously awarded and/or published my work: *ROOM Magazine, East Magazine, Maine Review, The Fiddlehead, Passengers Journal, The Massachusetts Review, HerStry, Electric Literature, The Normal School, Streetlight Magazine, Beyond Words Magazine, Columbia Journal, Sunspot Literary Journal, Harvard Review, Stonecoast Review, RFD Magazine, The Sun Magazine, CRAFT, Rubbertop Review,* TSR *The Southampton Review, Patterson Literary Review, The East Hampton Star, The Rumpus, Beyond Queer Words Anthology, The Arlington Literary Jornal, The Bangalore Review, Slippery Elm Literary Journal, Tiny Seed Journal, Dash Literary Journal, Detour Ahead Magazine, Wingless Dreamer, Mom Egg Review, Hartskill Review, Incluvie, Glint Literary Journal, AudioFile Magazine, Iowa Review, North American Review.*

Thank you to the supportive community my spouse and I landed in five years ago knowing absolutely no one or where to buy decent bread... particularly Alva G., Ty T., Holly R., Andrew Q., Baylee and

Quinn, Marna, Jess C., Anthony A., Vera G., Marcia G., Deborah G., Dana R., Liz L., Alexa, Kass, Brian and Jodi Z., Norbert, Michael R., Carsten, Martha and Steve N., Verna S., Judy D., Wanderson, Tracy R., and especially Susan K. and Steven S. (& Nancy), who really made and make so much possible.

Thanks to Jill K. for the trifecta: literary pal, pal pal, and occasional lifesaver. And to Pat A., Brittany K., Angie E., Varinder S., Stavros M., Tara C., for keeping me in the game.

Thanks to the support from my friends and colleagues at *The Rumpus*— I have boundless respect for all of you and it's inspirational to exist within a community such as this. Shout outs to my water cooler buddies Annelies Z., Addedayo A., and Robbie M. and to Roxane and Debbie for (literally) saving the joint.

Thank you to my in-laws Arlene and Alan for heterogeneous generosities and myriad examples of leading unapologetically creative lives and especially Arlene who believed in, encouraged, and championed my writing earlier than perhaps anyone including me.

Thank you to my son Kaden for being staggeringly brave about gender.

Thank you to my son Matteo for engaging beyond the page and sharing your endless hotel and flight plans.

This book would not exist in its most evolved form without the expertise, sophistication and benevolence of those at *Driftwood Press*. Massive thanks to Sara Moore Wagner, your god-is-in-the-details edits elevate, and your insistence I change the title (twice) made the difference. Also thank you, in particular, to James McNulty, Founder and Publisher for going above and further above (including writing me back on weekends even though you officially don't.)

Thank you to Cassie Mannes Murray at Pine State Publicity... you said, "We'll have fun!" and you were right!

More than two decades have passed since Beatrice came into my life, evolving it in ways revealing themselves daily. The morning coffee in bed only scratches a thick surface of my gratitude for our partnership... so thank you here as well.

Photography: Beatrice Alda

J Brooke's work is known for exploring gender, family, and the incendiary combination of the two. With this, their first book, they deliver candid commentary on a unique gender journey. Born intrinsically male, assigned female at birth, and raised in affluent dysfunction in New York City, their gender expression attempted male, cis straight female, and cis gay female before embracing a nonbinary identity. Living without surgical or hormonal interventions, their struggle to find authentic place and sustain it becomes the wrestling match this book offers a front row seat to, traversing female anatomy, friendship, suicide, family, testosterone, politics, packers, social media, motherhood, royalty, natural phenomena, cancer, marriage, and the pope. Brooke is Prose Reviews Editor at *The Rumpus*, and lives in New England with their beautiful spouse Beatrice.

OTHER DRIFTWOOD PRESS TITLES

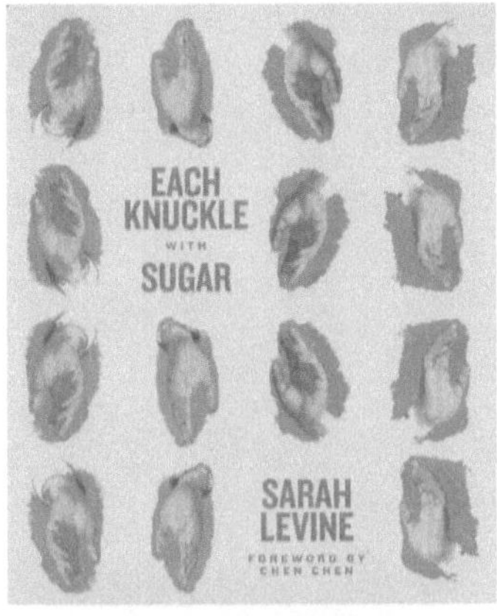

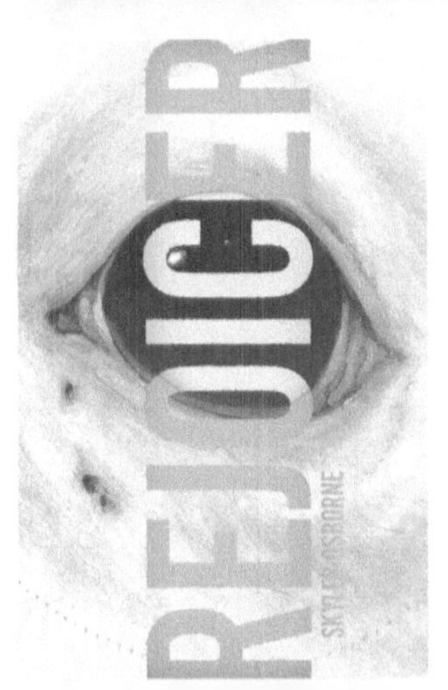

www.ingramcontent.com/pod-product-compliance
Lightning Source LLC
Chambersburg PA
CBHW021129070726
47591CB00014B/2078

* 9 7 8 1 9 4 9 0 6 5 4 3 5 *